Buried Treasure

Heather Hammonds

Contents

Rigby

What Are Gemstones?

For thousands of years, people have been collecting gemstones. There are lots of different gemstones. Many are very beautiful, and some are very rare.

Most gemstones are **minerals** that have formed into **crystals**.

Mineral gemstones

Some gemstones are **fossils**.
They are the remains
of living things!

Gemstones are
cut and polished
into different
shapes and sizes.

Sometimes they are
made into jewelry.

3

Mineral Gemstones

Long ago, mineral gemstones formed deep in special types of rock. **Prospectors** hunt for these rocks. Then mines are dug to collect the gemstones.

Gemstones have been found on the ground, by cliffs, or near river beds.

Sometimes wind and rain wash mineral gemstones out of the rocks where they formed.

Fossil Gemstones

Gemstones that are formed from the remains of living things are often buried under rock and soil.

Amber

In some parts of the world, these types of gemstones can be found in the sea. Sometimes they are washed up on the beach.

From Gemstones to Gems

Rough gemstones can look very beautiful.
They can be unusual shapes and colors.

But when
gemstones are
cut and polished,
they look even
more beautiful.
They become gems!

Some gemstones are very **valuable**. **Precious** gems, like rubies, can be cut from them.

Rubies are very valuable.

Other gemstones are not so valuable. They are easier to find or not as beautiful.

Quartz is not as valuable as rubies.

Mining for

Mining for gemstones is hard work. Miners use machines and tools to dig away rock and earth.

An underground mine

Underground mines are made up of tunnels and caverns. They are dug deep into the earth.

Open pit mines are cut into the surface of the earth. They make large holes in the land.

An open pit mine

Gemstones

At some mines, rock and earth are drilled and blasted from the ground.

Trucks carry the rock and earth to **processing plants**.

At the processing plants, the rock and earth are crushed. Special machines sort the gemstones from the crushed rock and earth.

Cutting and polishing gems from gemstones is delicate work. A person who cuts and polishes gems is called a **lapidary**.

Cut and Polish

After gemstones have been sorted from the crushed rock and earth, they are cut into smaller shapes. They are now ready to be given a final cut and polish and to be turned into gems.

The gemstone is cut with a special saw. Grinding and sanding wheels are used to shape the gemstone.

The gemstone is polished until it glitters and shines. It has become a gem!

After

Before

Some gems have many small flat surfaces called **facets**.

Some gems are polished into round or square shapes.

Did You Know...

that the weight of a gem is measured in **carats**? One carat = 0.2 grams

Diamonds

Diamonds are very precious gems. Diamonds can be many different colors. The most valuable diamonds are called white diamonds. They are clear, and have no color at all.

Diamonds are used to make beautiful jewelry.

Diamonds are the hardest material on Earth!

Some diamonds are not good enough to be cut and polished into gems, so they are used in other ways. Because diamonds are so hard, they can be used to cut and grind many things.

Saws and cutting blades can be diamond-tipped. This makes them strong and sharp.

Jewelers use diamond-tipped blades when working with diamonds.

Rubies and Sapphires

Rubies and sapphires are very beautiful gems. They come from the same type of gemstone, but they are different colors.

Rubies are different shades of red.

Ruby

Sapphires can be many colors, such as yellow, pink, orange, and purple. The most well-known sapphires are blue.

Blue sapphire

Colored sapphires

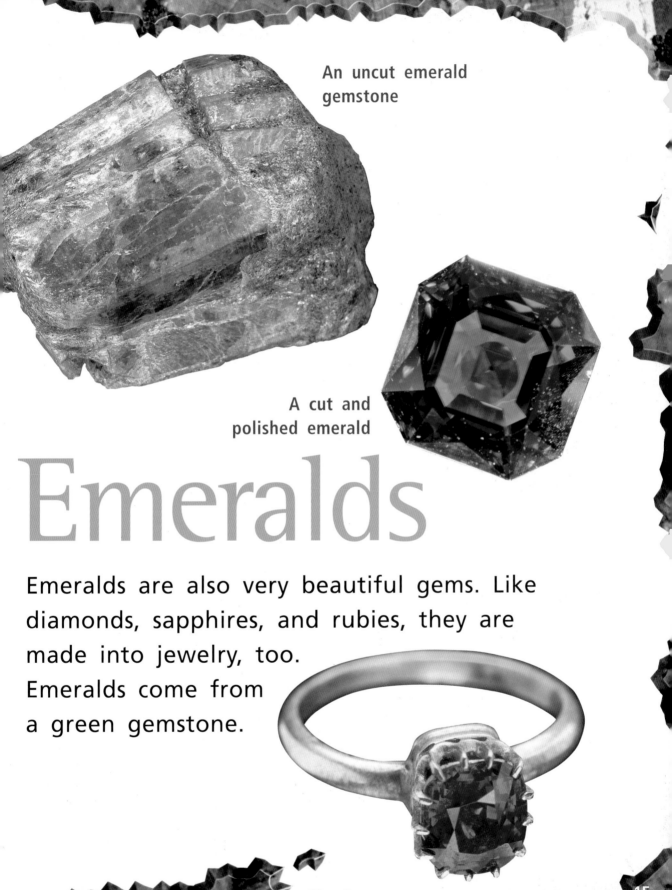

An uncut emerald gemstone

A cut and polished emerald

Emeralds

Emeralds are also very beautiful gems. Like diamonds, sapphires, and rubies, they are made into jewelry, too. Emeralds come from a green gemstone.

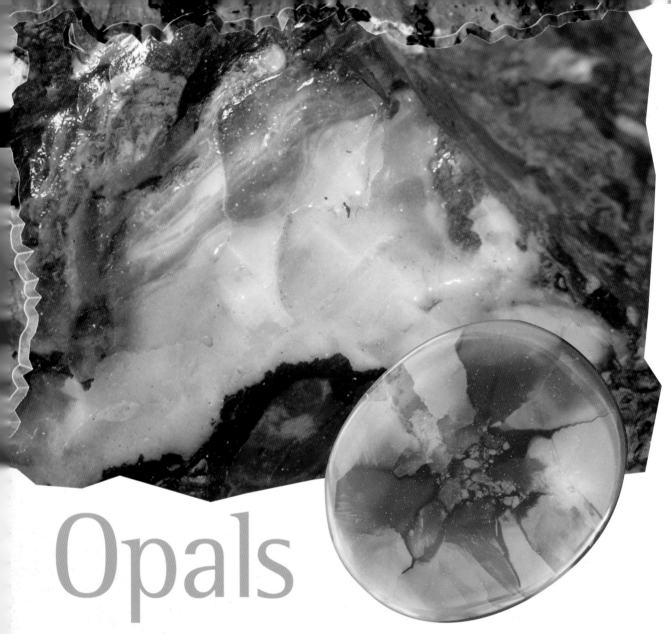

Opals

Opals glitter when moved around, showing many beautiful colors.

Opals are not as hard or strong as other gems. They crack or chip easily. When lapidaries cut and polish opals, they must be careful not to damage them.

Opal gemstones were
formed millions of
years ago. Some
opals form in the
shape of plants
and animals from
long ago!

This opal is in the
shape of a shell.

Over a very long time, the
opal replaced parts of the dead
plant or animal. These opal fossils
are very valuable.

This opal is in the shape
of an ancient animal's jaw.

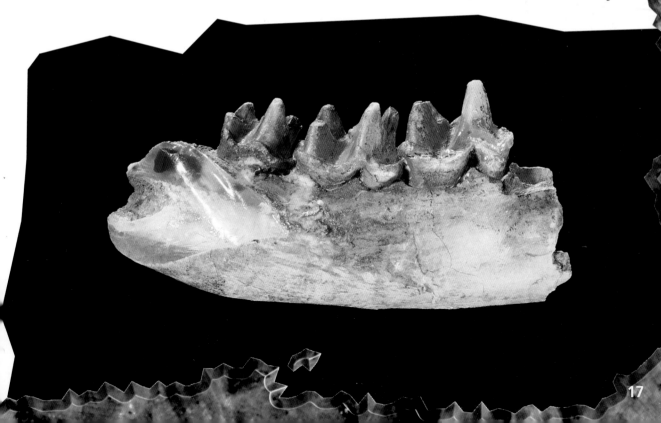

Amber

Amber is millions of years old.

Amber is the fossilized resin of trees that lived millions of years ago.

Small insects and plants sometimes stuck to **resin** as it dripped from the trees.

Today, we can still see the insects and plants inside some pieces of amber.

Jet

Jet is a special type of black coal. Coal is a type of rock. Coal formed millions of years ago from the remains of dead plants.

Jet is carved and polished into beads and jewelry.

Synthetic Gemstones

Today, many gemstones can be made in **laboratories**. They are called **synthetic** gemstones. Synthetic gemstones are made from the same minerals as natural gemstones, but instead of forming in rock, these gemstones are formed in special **furnaces**. Gems are cut from them.

Synthetic gems are much cheaper than natural gems. They are not as rare or as special as natural gems, but they are still beautiful.

Synthetic gems look the same as natural gems to most people. But expert **gemologists** can tell the difference between them by using special instruments.

Natural gems often have tiny marks and pieces of other minerals inside them. Sometimes, synthetic gems have tiny bubbles inside them.

Birthstones

Long ago, people believed gemstones had magical powers. Some gemstones were used in medicines. Others were worn as good luck charms.

Some gemstones are connected with different months of the year. They are called birthstones.

Today, many people like to wear gems connected to the month they were born.

Month	Gemstone	
January	garnet	
February	amethyst	
March	aquamarine	
April	diamond	
May	emerald	
June	pearl	
July	ruby	
August	peridot	
September	sapphire	
October	opal	
November	topaz	
December	turquoise	

Glossary

carats the units of weight that gems are measured by

crystals objects made of many tiny minerals, joined together in regular patterns

facets small flat surfaces, cut into gems

furnaces huge hot ovens

fossils the remains of animals and plants that lived millions of years ago

gemologists people who study gems and gemstones

laboratories places where science experiments are done

lapidary a person who cuts and polishes gemstones

minerals tiny parts of rock and earth that are not formed from animals or plants

precious most valuable

processing plants factories where rock and earth are sorted to collect gemstones

prospectors people who search the land for valuable rocks and minerals

resin a sticky material made by some plants, such as pine trees

synthetic not made in nature, but made by people

valuable something that is worth a lot of money

Index